To order additional copies of this book, contact:
Xlibris
844-714-8691
www.Xlibris.com
Orders@Xlibris.com

ISBN: Softcover   978-1-4257-5670-3
         Hardcover   978-1-4257-5673-4

Library of Congress Control Number: 2007904005

Print information available on the last page

Rev. date: 12/15/2020

GIFT BOOK

to

_____

from

_____

Finally, brethren, whatsoever things are true, whatsoever things are
honest,
whatsoever things are just, whatsoever things are pure,
whatsoever things are lovely, whatsoever things are of good report;
If there be any virtue, and if there be any praise, think on these things.

—Phil. 4:8 (KJV)

INTRODUCTION

Within the pages of this book, I have written some of my essential lifetime lessons. It is said that you are the author of your life, so you should make your story interesting.

This is a book of creative, witty, inspiring, and motivating thoughts. This is also a book that will bring colour to your thoughts as you reflect upon life's caprices.

These thoughts are also provocative and can be used by speech-makers and writers who need pertinent truths to illustrate their points or just to add ingredients to life.

It is my hope that as you read, you will be inspired to greatness, not just meandering through life but finding purpose in every day.

LOVE

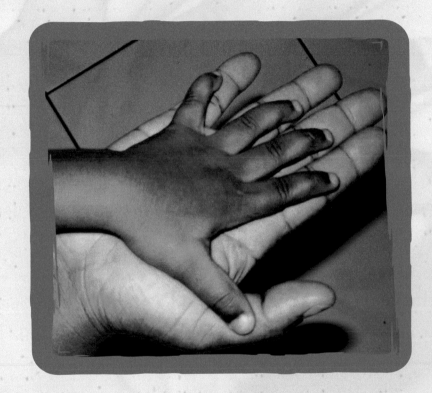

Love has hands.
Love always seeks expression.

~ J. D. Gordon

WEALTH

Aim to be rich — poverty is more expensive.

~ J. D. Gordon

SMILES

Wear a smile—it is cheap, but its lasting effect is beyond value. A little smile can change the weather.

~ J. D. Gordon

ENVIRONMENT

Find your soil or die.
Your state of mind is reflected in your environment.
Whatever you wish to see done in your environment, begin to do it.

~ J. D. Gordon

MUSIC

Music is an inexhaustible art—the more you have, the more you want. There is always a new sound to be heard from music you have heard many times before.

~ J. D. Gordon

ATTITUDE

Those who have the best and those who make the best of what they have are one and the same.

~ J. D. Gordon

ENVIRONMENT

By simply changing your mind, you can alter your environment, your health, and your peace of mind.

~ J. D. Gordon

PATIENCE

There are two main things in life that teach me the virtue of patience—a child and an old car.

~ J. D. Gordon

SUCCESS

It is not so much your physical position or location that brings success but more of your mental condition.

~ J. D. Gordon

LOVE

Love is like the engine of a motorcar; it either drives you or shuts you down.
The one who loves the most hurts the most.
To love someone does not mean liking every little thing about them.
Love gives, so give love.

~ J. D. Gordon

MUSIC

Music is in everything we do — our lives are but phrases and rhythms that dictate our every move and routine.
Music inspires changes — a change of attitude or a change of mind.

~ J. D. Gordon

LIFE

It is better to cruise rather than to keep rushing through life—after all, you will not receive a prize for finishing first.

Your life can be like a musical chair—you keep going around in circles until the music stops.

~ J. D. Gordon

INSPIRATION AND DREAMS

Inspire me to greatness—let me dream, create, and do the impossible.
Only you truly want to see your dreams come true

~ J. D. Gordon

FAITH

Faith makes you look silly at times as it defies the very laws of nature.

~ J. D. Gordon

SECURITY

Make your nest before you mate.

~ J. D. Gordon

FORGIVENESS

*Unforgiveness hurts the unforgiver
more than anyone else.*

~ J. D. Gordon

DESIRES

*Music,
the heart beat
of God*

When your desires change,
your focus will change.

~ J. D. Gordon

LIFE

Life isn't a race, it's a journey; so enjoy each stop, each delay, each traffic jam, and each scenery. But most of all, treasure every lesson learnt.

If I slow down, then I may last a little longer.

~ J. D. Gordon

PASSION

Your commitment and passion attract others to you.

~ J. D. Gordon

THOUGHTS

*Poison is in everything—in speech, in drink,
and even in your thoughts.*

~ J. D. Gordon

ANGER

Control your emotions or you could make a bad decision. Anger, if conceived, can consume you like fire.

~ J. D. Gordon

SERVICE

*E*ach of us has an innate desire to serve and to be served;
our actions are therefore subtle and palpable indicators of
who we serve and who is serving us.

~ J. D. Gordon

LISTEN

A good listener listens with the heart as he also hear what isn't said.

~ J. D. Gordon

REBELLION

Where there is rebellion, there are many rulers.

~ J. D. Gordon

SUNSET

The sun sets every day, yet each setting of the sun looks new, different, and picturesque.

~ J. D. Gordon

PERCEPTION

One reason the grass seems greener on the other side is that you are too far to see the patches.

~ J. D. Gordon

HEART

Follow your heart but remember your responsibilities.

~ J. D. Gordon

GOD

If God seems far, perhaps you have moved.
For this generation to experience the power of
God, the godly people must show it.

~ J. D. Gordon

THE CHURCH

The Church opens its arms to a sinner who becomes a Christian, but oftentimes drives away a Christian who becomes a sinner.

~ J. D. Gordon

CAUTION

Read the signs carefully.

~ J. D. Gordon

GRATEFULNESS

*We take for granted the things or people
on which we can depend.*

~ J. D. Gordon

POVERTY

Who knows why we often scoff at the poor?

~ J. D. Gordon

LIFE

It took me all my thirty years to realize that I don't have to understand everything in life.

~ J. D. Gordon

MARRIAGE

A man at the head of a successful marriage is far more successful than the CEO of a profitable multinational company.

~ J. D. Gordon

INJUSTICE

What is considered wrong or right sometimes depends on the person who did it.

~ J. D. Gordon

OVERBURDENED

Every time you feel overburdened, stop, refuel, and go again.

~ J. D. Gordon

DILIGENCE

Seest thou a man diligent in his business? He shall stand before kings; he shall not stand before mean men.

~ Proverbs 22:29 (KJV)

HOT-TEMPER

Do not make friends with a hot-tempered man, do not associate with one easily angered, or you may learn his ways and get yourself ensnared.

~ Proverbs 22:24–25 (NIV)

VISION

*W*here there is no vision, the people perish: but he that keepeth the law, happy is he.

~ Proverbs 29:18 (KJV)

YOUTH

It is good for a man that he bear the yoke in his youth.

~ Lamentations 3:27 (NKJ)

ADVICE

A fool will always find someone more foolish to advise him.

Don't call an alligator a big-mouth until you have passed him.

~ Jamaican saying

CHARACTER

*All of us are like sponge—when squeezed,
we reveal what is on the inside.*

~ J. D. Gordon

CHILDREN

A child mirrors its environment.

~ J. D. Gordon

WORRY

If you keep worrying about your life, you will miss the meaning of life.

~ J. D. Gordon

APPRECIATION

If *you believe no one loves and appreciates you, wait until you die.*

~ J. D. Gordon

FREEDOM

*We crave the people and things
which allow us to be who we really are*

~ J. D. Gordon

REGRETS

Many mistakes you will make and live to regret, but only one, others will regret that you didn't live.

~ J. D. Gordon

DISCIPLINE

A youngster's heart is filled with foolishness,
but physical discipline will drive it far away.

~ Proverbs 22:15 (NLT)

CHANGES

Seasons change to make new, so why shouldn't you?

~ J. D. Gordon

APOLOGY

An apology is an honorable thing – it is a wonder that not many noble men do apologize.

~ J. D. Gordon

Photos of Jamaican sceneries were taken by:
Jermaine D Gordon   Melesha P Gordon
Jervis Johnson

Photos of Canada were taken by:
Gary Pillon

Author's photo taken by:
Pugh's Colour Lab

All paintings were done by:
Peter Peart

To order this Cd:
    Visit: www.dubtunes.com or email: jermainedg@hotmail.com

Spirit led Music for those moments of meditation, devotion and celebration.
Played at the pulse of the Holy Spirit, every note and chord inspires the
heart to true worship.
If you desire to have God's presence in your car, home or office, and to have your soul enriched then this makes good listening.

Printed in the United States
By Bookmasters